Can Your Dog Meow?

Regina Allen Parker

Illustrations by Demi DiPiazza

To order additional copies of this book, contact:
Xlibris
1-888-795-4274
www.Xlibris.com
Orders@Xlibris.com

This Book is DeDicateD to my three sons, D'AnDre, D'AnDrew, anD Darrian. They all graDuateD from BriDgeport High School in BriDgeport, West Virginia. It is my wish for my sons to strive to Do their Best with the talents that GoD has given to each of them anD to make this worlD a Better Place!

With All My Love,

Mom

No, my dog, he cannot meow

Because he is not a cat,

But what my dog can do at the park

Is bark, and bark, and bark!

No, my dog, he cannot meow
But his bark is really loud
Do not be afraid when my dog is barking
He may just be barking at the cloud.

No, my dog, he cannot meow
But he can wag his tail with glee
He wags his tail when he is happy
Then he jumps all over me!

No, my dog, he cannot meow
But he can fetch a ball or two
And if you throw it far away
He will bring it back to you!

6

No, my dog, he cannot meow
But he can poop and make it smell
And when you walk right pass my dog
You can really, really tell.

7

No, my dog, he cannot meow

But he can bury a bone really quick

He will dig up the grass to hide all his stash

Because he is really slick!

No, my dog, he cannot meow

But he knows how to make a rubble

When he is caught doing something wrong

He knows he will be in trouble!

No, my dog, he cannot meow

And neither does he hiss,

But he likes to lick my face a lot

With a juicy and sloppy kiss!

No, my dog, he cannot meow,

But he loves to get yummy sweets

He will flip and perform a trick or two

If you give him some yum, yum treats!

No, my dog, he cannot meow

But he follows commands everyday

When he thinks to chase a cat away

I simply tell him to stay!

No, my dog, he cannot meow

But he can warn me of unwanted danger

This makes me love my dog even more

Because he protects me from unwelcomed strangers.

About the Illustrator

Demi DiPiazza is a sophomore at BHS, Bridgeport, West Virginia. She was given the opportunity to illustrate, "Can Your Dog Meow?" When author Regina Allen Parker reached out to the BHS Art Club, DiPiazza was ecstatic to have the chance to take on a project that would benefit her in her future goal of becoming a cartoon animator. DiPiazza experience with the book has been nothing but enjoyable! Outside of school, DiPiazza likes to draw, of course, and write; she is even working on illustrating her own Webcomics! She is also involved in theater and has worked on shows produced by the BHS Theater Department since her freshman year.

Special thanks to Demi DiPiazza of Bridgeport High School, Bridgeport, West Virginia, for providing the illustrations for this book. Likewise, thanks to the BHS Arts Department managed by Miss Courtney Rankin. Through a class competition given by Miss Rankin to show off student's arts and abilities, DiPiazza was hand-selected by author Parker based upon the talent shown in her artwork. A lot of time, collaboration, and hard work has gone into this book and I am proud of the results.

—Regina Allen Parker

About the Author

Regina Allen Parker is a first-time author, born and raised in Memphis, Tennessee, and currently living in Bridgeport, West Virginia. Parker's desire to publish a children's book was inspired by various children authors with the attitude that she could write a book too. Since graduating from Fairmont State University in May 2014 with a Bachelor of Arts degree, Parker focused her enthusiasm, creativity, and energy on writing her very first children's book and now her republication with illustrations. In May 2013, Parker joined the Literacy Volunteers of Harrison County (a United Way agency) in Clarksburg, West Virginia as a board member. When it comes to literacy, she believes that reading together should encourage parents to give their children love and attention and to make reading easy and fun!